Take Something When You Go

Dawn Leas

Winter Goose
PUBLISHING
where words take flight

Winter Goose Publishing
45 Lafayette Road #114
North Hampton, NH 03862

www.wintergoosepublishing.com
Contact Information: info@wintergoosepublishing.com

Take Something When You Go

COPYRIGHT © 2016 by Dawn Leas

First Edition, 2016, March

Cover Design by Winter Goose Publishing
Cover Photo by Dawn Leas
Typesetting by Odyssey Books

ISBN: 978-1-941058-43-5

Published in the United States of America

"Tell all the truth but tell it slant."

—Emily Dickinson

.

Contents

For my parents

Explorer

I dive off the plains of a map
      like water over a fall,
          a snowy egret migration,
          an amber leaf letting go,
          a wish, or a prayer.
Almost a dream. Almost real.
Always moving, toward and away.

Ice Melt

My sons end their days
on rooftops in a semi-circle of friends
mulling over what comes
after academic hiccups
and break-ups,
what life is like after college
and before thirty.

But back in 1990,
when we were supposed
to finish college, find jobs,
be settled before settling in
with one another, our oldest
was brand new.

I fought to prove
we would be the one out of two
who stayed together. I played
June Cleaver—cleaned and ironed,
dressed up for your company's Christmas party,
kept your dinner warm on nights
you worked late.
At the end of long
days, I knelt for you. I prayed.

I nurtured
strict bed times, tuned
into educational TV, bundled toddlers

in snowsuits to trek to story time
at the Children's Library, slipped
my stretch-marked body into the cool
water of the Dunmore Y,
so our boys could learn to swim.

Sleepless hours seeped
deep into bones and midnight tears
rolled onto tops of bald heads
while cracked and bleeding
nipples screamed.

I became so thirsty,
almost dehydrated,
when the well ran dry
and I snapped words that stung
at you, at them.

The boys watched
afternoons of *Barney*
and *Thomas the Tank Engine*
because I was too tired
to play Candyland or Go Fish.

Our twelve-hour days
at the office and at home created
a chasm we alternately traversed,
then ignored until it almost
swallowed us.

I spent winters at the picture window
watching storms descend
over Montage Mountain,
and bury my dreams
under layers of ice.
Days and nights lapped one another
into years and fast forwarded to decades.
Words lost their sting,
and memory forgot.

Our sons learned
that ice melts faster in the city
than it does in the mountains.

Dry Spell

Tumbleweeds chase scorpions
across the cracked river bed.

We build camps on opposite plateaus.

Words echo
across a crag-filled abyss.

A dust storm flings
      my name,
      your name.

From up here
the canyon
is an abandoned graveyard.

Winds shift.

Our bridge of rope and wood
sways.

Still,
no rain.

View from Canyon Lake Overlook Near Top of Superstition Mountains

Sharing a double bed
with sister while storm
raged in living room.

Summer thick as a bayou
at aunt's house
reading biographies.

Four generations stroll
on Bourbon Street.

Love's Baby Soft
sparking Aramis
in Chevy Impala back seat.

Eating mac & cheese
and listening to Michael
Jackson's *Off the Wall*
with best friend at two a.m.

A magnetic first
glance. Two babies
with peach-fuzz heads
grown by lightning-fast
years into adults.

Over two decades
of marriage, three careers,
history inked in Celtic
swirls, the sun, moon, and stars.

Purple stretch marks
fade to pink.
Sun spots sprouting,
ocean salt tears,
middle-age waist,
vertical worry line above
left eye,
fear heavy as wet snow.

Now, body is a sturdy saguaro,
spirit opens like a desert road,
no end

in sight.

Sunday Morning

Early spring drums
on the tin roof above,
and its steady rhythm leaves
as quickly as it arrives.

She burrows deeper
into the folds of the indigo quilt
her grandmother hand-stitched
before she was born.

Soft whispers
rise from below,
a chair scrapes tile floor. Creak
of stair after stair, the cat
runs down to catch crinkled ball of paper.

Coffee pot gurgle, hiss of bacon,
muffled laughter, scissors
slicing paper, quick
peel of tape. Utensils

shuffle, stoneware friction
against granite counter.

A moment of quiet.

Bare feet padding on hardwood.
Creak of stairs, giggles, *shh* . . .

bedroom door opens. Pair
of preschoolers jumps onto bed.
With a feast and gifts laid
at her feet, tradition unfolds.

Empty Nest

The spring before our youngest
took flight, a robin built a nest—
a tangle of twigs, leaves,
and grass—in the Christmas wreath
hanging on the front door.

She found refuge
among the new buds of the oak tree
each time I opened the door
to check on the eggs.

One night, I stood against the door
and heard staccato chirps. I eased
the door open and stood
on tiptoes to peer into the nest.

Three babies with wet, matted fur,
their mouths opened skyward,
ravenous.

As soon as they broke through
their bright blue shells, she fed
and mothered, prepping
them for flight.

Inside the house, I unpacked college life—
laundered towels and folded sheets—
repacked and stored containers

in the hall closet. I tagged toys and video games
for a yard sale, made Salvation Army piles, priced
international flights, crossed days off on the calendar

while the babies chirped for food
and learned to fly.
While debris of nest life overflowed
onto the wreath and door.

May brought silence,
a heap of blue
and tufts of feathers
littering the welcome mat.

By August, the silence
migrated into the house.

Handwashing

That summer
sizzled at first,
then quickly cooled,
like a branding iron
plunged into water.

A cold
sent me to bed
where my fever
drenched
the cotton sheets.

He came
and went from the bedroom,
drew the shades,
placed ice water
on the bedside table.

When I woke,
I wondered
what was real as he
massaged my hands
one at a time
with a cold washcloth
until the fibers turned lukewarm.

He kneaded my palms
with his fingertips
until the fever rose
out of me like a phoenix
and as night overtook
day, my skin cooled.

We changed the sheets
and slept in the same bed
for the first time in days.
He brought me back to life again.

Empty Cars

You walk into the kitchen,
shaking the February cold
from your coat,
flecks of snow melt in your hair.

I stir a pot of sauce, its steam carries past Sunday
dinners at my parents', kids playing Go Fish

in the family room. You lean against the island
and cross your arms. I'm slicing cloves of garlic

when you say that empty cars, dark and idle,
in the driveway, make you sad sometimes.

I stop chopping and for the first time since the boys left,
I see you, really know you. I no longer question

what keeps a marriage together through years of northern
winters, no sun, only grey clouds, slick ice,

what moves people past the fringe into longing again.

City Dwellers

I raised city dwellers
deep in suburban trenches
bordering farmland and forest
with a state park as a playground.

Whine of Saturday morning lawnmowers,
sting of weed killer,
houses buttoned up with central air,
block parties and flashlight tag.

I said no to walking to friends' houses
on county roads, no sidewalks,
a berm of rocky ditches.

We spent their childhood in an SUV
to and from school,
piano lessons, soccer and golf matches.

After bedtime stories, I whispered prayers,
                    please find your way.
I packed lunch notes,
                    you can go far.

Now they travel I-80 through the Delaware Water Gap,
its mountains russet across my home state
through the Lincoln Tunnel to Washington Square Park,
over the GW bridge, north on the Henry Hudson
to a Hughes Street off-campus apartment.

Subway maps are decoded,
routes memorized for the NQR,
the 123, Metro North.

They wander the streets
from Alphabet City to the Upper West Side
and see bands I never heard of
at Webster Hall and Terminal 5.

They text and call home.
There's no reason to return, I say.
You've found your way. I'll find mine.

EastWest

I am waking up with first-day jitters
while you are winding down,
off-balance with jet-lag, street
signs you can't yet read outside the window.

I am waking up to lesson plans
and missed homework assignments
while you are winding down,
practicing character strokes,
eating fried rice bought at a street vendor
just beyond the back gate of campus.

I am waking up to sunrise memories
of the day you were born
while you are winding down
from a day of climbing dunes,
riding a camel, and making bread
with Tibetan monks.

I am waking up to snow in October
while you are winding down
at an ex-pat jazz club, mocking
those drinking pumpkin beer
like they are on the western side of the world.

I am waking up to the idea that you
are not a baby, a boy, or a teenager,
and now you are winding down

writing final papers and packing
your bags to fly south,
north, east, and finally, west again.

Red Earrings

A tow-headed toddler climbs
a steel stool in a vintage boutique.
Kneeling in tiny Levi's and nubuck saddle shoes,
he leans on the glass countertop
to twirl a constellation of earrings,
       so many shining stars, an orbit of possibility.

Standing behind him, her arms a safety net,
his grandmother points to silver studs, gold teardrops.
He shakes his head, hair brushing tips of eyelashes.
His eyes are amber orbs searching until finally finding
a burst of brilliant red beads
       dangling on a simple twist of wire.

This is how he sees his mother—
a red planet, the center of his small universe.

A lifetime later, when he's light-years away,
       and his mother wears the red earrings,
this is how she sees him—
an experienced explorer
       who knows to look to the sky to find his way home.

First Year

We pack the car with boxes,
        bags, suitcases,

eighteen photos (curly-haired toddler to long-haired teen),
        Port Imperiale Ferry Schedule,

Martz bus tickets, color-coded
        subway map, new running shoes,

a hand-written list of favorite New York
        places, gift cards to MOMA, the Met,

grandmother's lasagna on ice,
        a bag full of purple Skittles,

artist's tools—guitar, pens
        and pencils, a sketchbook—

The Great Gatsby, cell phone charger,
        laptop, change for the laundry,

extra-long sheets, R.E.M. and Bruce posters,
        iPod loaded with Elbow, The National,

Pearl Jam, U2, Doves . . . words left unsaid,
        a string of apologies, a bucket of promises,

years of life, advice, silent scenes from the past,
      the holding on and the letting go

wrapped tight in a prolonged good morning,
      then a long hug goodbye.

Slipstream

A response to Ryan's article on U2's Zooropa
turning twenty, July 2013

The year *Zooropa* was born
you were a fiery redhead.
The summer sweltered and we holed up
in our Cape Cod's family room,
curtains closed against sun.

Late at night, when you and your dad
were asleep, I nursed
your newborn brother and watched the "Numb" video.

Barely across the threshold of adulthood,
I dreamt out loud so you could live out loud,
     feel steady push of wind
     fly across water
     travel on land
     throw away the map
knowing uncertainty is the whoosh of a flame igniting.

Twenty years later, I am running laps
around our suburban sprawl with "Zooropa"
on repeat. From a distance, I see the three of you
washing cars in the driveway,
ruddy faces in July heat.

  What do you want?
     What do you want?
What do you want?

Facebook Status Updates, 2011

I love rainy Saturdays drenched, cloaked,
in slow motion. If I cry
during Winnie-the-Pooh trailers,
what's to come at end of August?
Over the moon for the Bronx,
it's fasten-your-seatbelt time
and one step closer to Shanghai.
These days revolve too quickly
for flight delays
and breakfast at Hibernia Diner.
I try to put right words
in right order, but can't get past clichés.
This will take some time,
but maybe, just maybe—
I can get used to an empty house.

Day Before Freshman Move-In

Her husband and son work in silence in the garage
surrounded by childhood leftovers—
a dusty bag of soccer balls,
trail bikes upside down on the wall,
old golf shoes tied together by spider webs.

Jazz streams from the iPod dock
on top of hose reel.

The father under the car
asks for tools with outstretched hand,
nails rimmed black, no words.

The son sits on concrete floor,
delivers wrench,
screwdriver,
paper towels.

Old oil streams into a collection pan
a black lake,
its surface like waves.

The son hovers over engine
and pours in clean oil,
a dropless, pristine delivery.

Inside the house,
she hunts and gathers

suitcases from the basement,
stacks storage bins in the piano room
to fill with toothpaste,
Clorox wipes, notebooks,
and mechanical pencils.

Sitting cross-legged on the floor,
she folds fresh towels
and extra-long twin sheets,
a comforter.

She remembers the day he was born:
another humid summer,
the nurse pushed her body weight into her,
apologized for the discomfort
but emphasized the necessity to deliver the placenta,
which slid out full-bodied red. The doctor
placed it in metal pan as gently as he
had handled her son minutes earlier.
It shimmied like a jellyfish
for just a few seconds
before settling into stillness.

Tomorrow, they will collect miles
on the interstate, station wagon's odometer
turning over and over as they speed
toward delivering their son again,
inches closer to her own deliverance.

Weight

Honey-oak shelves dip
under weight of things.
Black frames hold bald babies,
toddlers with curls and crew cuts,
preschool handprints, graduations.
Once neatly arranged, now askew
like wind-whipped branches.
Middle-school sculptures
live in the shadow of corners.
Books and photo albums held
up by clay bowls. Tiny mounds
of incense ash litter the mantle,
pottery teetering on its edge.
Several melted candles,
defeated. A painting of an empty
bench in a dark forest tilts left
just above fireplace. Tethered
to a flower vase, a deflating
balloon drifts. Whirls of dust
swirl. This just one wall
of one room of the house.

Imagine the rest
            after haste of leaving.
Imagine counting days,
            the wait for return.

Morse Code

When you whipped
a half-empty
water bottle

like a slider   across the driveway

I cried for the first time.

Not because you
seethed over
          laundry
          a forgotten bill
          the scratched car door
because you said you moved on.

That night I ran loops. The fireflies returned.

Orange exclamation points—

blink   dark   blink   run

          flash   flash   flash

a visual Morse code
dots

the heavy summer air.

History

You are filling your suitcase:
two pairs of running shoes, race hat,
and throwaway gloves when your phone vibrates.

The unexpected call electrifies your apron strings
and its current transposes his words into notes
tumbling from a trumpet
like his father playing "Amazing Grace"
or Bono singing "With or Without You."

For past lessons, he says *thank you.*
Future forecast of career and family, so sweet
like Godiva chocolate,
a sunrise run on a winter beach.

After the call ends, you race to pen his story,
then slide slip of paper into an Alice Munro collection
so years from today
when the conversation is forgotten
and he's far away, you can open the book
to remember
he is more like you than you ever imagined.

On His Twenty-Fourth Birthday

I run the levee along the river
that I spent decades running away from.

Men are fishing in water
that touches the middle of their chests.

Twenty-four years ago, I felt like I was wading
through water, a bottom
I couldn't reach.

As the contractions got stronger
I felt like I was being held underwater,
those middle-of-the-night hours
I waited in my room
for the nurse to bring him from the NICU.

I run by soccer fields where fourteen years ago
he sat on the sidelines
reading Harry Potter books
or drawing in a sketchbook
while his brother scored hat tricks.

I reach the turnaround and realize
it's been six years since I stood
in Kirby Park
watching his cross country meets,
five years since he graduated high school,
and three since he spent his birthday in China.

I slow to a walk at mile three
to write this poem. Today, the fall sun
is as hot as a still August afternoon.
Sweat rolls into my eyes.

I round the bend a quarter mile
from the end.
A prop plane descends
over the browning cornfield,
its shadow crosses my path
as it heads toward the runway.

I look ahead and see his
father sitting on a bench
under trees that have already
lost half of their leaves.

He's waiting for me
like he was thirty years
ago in the aisle of Costa Drugs,
almost twenty-five years ago at the alter
in Scared Hearts of Jesus and Mary,
waiting with me twenty-four years ago
in that hospital room,
and countless nights at home
while I chased ghosts downstream.

Vacation

One spring, I flew south alone,
above the topography of our relationship:
mountainous, creviced and stitched.

Solitary days spent sitting on the beach
begging the waveless Gulf for words.

Nights spent sleeping single in a queen bed,
its luxurious emptiness my cocoon.

How I settled into a solo routine.
A morning walk, clothes, shoes, and books

strewn across the room, reading and writing.
Words tumbled to the page like surf to shore.

I regenerated in voluminous swaths of silence,
a patchwork quilt pieced two generations ago.

Then, a northern arrival on an afternoon flight.
Anticipation bubbled. The tidying began.

I moved piles and emptied a drawer,
lined up shoes to make a path on my way
to becoming one half of a pair once again.

Reconciliation

We waded through the bayous of my childhood—
black water, a witch's stew churned below a canopy

of arthritic branches. Veins of cypress and tupelo
were mountains to climb. At ground level, no guide,

only ethereal tendrils of light. No guide, we moved
by touch. Humidity heaved a sigh and mildewed air

squeezed our lungs into spontaneous words.
At midnight, you played notes I hadn't yet heard.

Thrum of jazzy bass migrated from the French
Quarter, mood music for the foreign territory

we were now traversing. In the late hours
of a melancholy night we danced with stillness.

Not worrying about cottonmouth venom, piercing
pain of bite, we swam together day and night,

then day again in those chicory waters deep
enough to tread, face to face, lips close.

By summer's waning days, I learned sometimes
to move forward you must go back.

The Morning Wakes Up

High in the pines,
mourning doves woo.

We circle Sugar Magnolia
twice with the emerging sun,
breathe in the silence.

Pelicans fish on Blue Juniper,
and we linger at the edge of the pond,
snap pictures to send home.

Our conversation curves around
Burnt Sienna Circle.

A place for roots
takes shape in the bend
of Old Mahogany Court.

Words, planned and unexpected,
slip quickly from our lips
in this walled hamlet.

The day after celebrating twenty-four years,
we sprint together
into the Wild Forest.

Don't look back,
        the pelicans plead.

Late morning rocks
the doves to sleep.

Bonfire

I walk the dirt road
and dodge muddied holes
in the dark.

The bonfire glow rises
above treetops, smoke
spirals into the fall sky
as dead leaves huddle at the edge
of the road.

Ahead,
the porch light illuminates
his still shadow on the swing.
Miles Davis music
floats through the screen.

This house is still,
like church before sunrise Mass.
Rooms that once absorbed
echoes of Saturday morning
cartoons and the tussle of boys
are hollow spaces now.

He reaches out. *Coffee's on.*
The fire's lit. I say nothing
as he stands and we walk together,
his hand on the small of my back.

Air is turning, I think. *Soon,*
We'll know the bite of winter.

Carpet Cleaning

After the house empties
and the leaves change,
we assess the *I'll-get-to-it-next-weekend* chores.

Walls adorned
with scuff marks and nail pops,
the faded front door,
and uneven sidewalks.

In the family room, we map
the seasons in the carpet,
a connect-the-dots of our life—
children with cleats,
pets, and juice spills.

Can it be saved? you ask.

I study the mosaic of dirt, stain, and spot-treated circles.

Anything can be saved, I say.
But, how badly do you want it?

Date Night

On the eve of fleeing back to the city,
our sons make a family dinner.
They peel and cut potatoes, carefully lower
them into a fryer. Hot oil spits.
Burgers fry—
rare for them, well-done for me.
Smoke whorls from the pan.

Watching them takes me back two decades
to your grandmother's basement
kitchen where she left our meatloaf,
fries, and mac & cheese
covered on top of a still warm stove
before leaving for her Saturday-night
bowling league.

Her turn-of-the-century stairway,
papered with tobacco smoke
and coal dust, was so narrow
I had to walk in front of you,
so steep you placed your hands
on my hips to keep me
from falling back.

After sex and before dinner,
you would take a bath
in the claw-foot tub.
I sat on the brown
shag carpet leaning against the paneled
wall. We talked about life
after college, jobs we'd like to have,
cars to buy. The water level bobbed
as you sank below the surface
to rinse your hair.

Turning Forty

On duty for neighborhood watch,
leafy eyes meander
over a thick diagonal pattern,
cut twice. An ornamental pear
peers through darkened windows

and catches a glimpse of life
lived on other side of the street.

Thin branches stretch through
pane and pick their way along
a guitar riff late on

Saturday night. The tree scribbles
notes as jazz trumpet picks up beat
of a family in tune.

Drums keep pace with life
on the move.

Washed Out to Sea

Watching news coverage of Hurricane Sandy

Just a year before the storm,
my husband and I stood
on the boardwalk of my childhood,
its beach a thick blanket unfolding
to rim of calmer water.

Now, we sit in our family room
over a hundred miles away
and watch images flicker on the screen:
Lower Manhattan under water,
broken boards tossed
like matchsticks, amusement rides
drowning just off shore.

This isn't the blue-eyed, sunny Sandy
who made me fall in love with love
in 1978. The one who taught me
how to catch and keep
a boyfriend while she sang
"You're the One That I Want"
and "Hopelessly Devoted to You."

There's nothing calm about this one's green eye,
quick to steal what others loved.
She hoards heirlooms,
sparks gas explosions,
howls long into the night,
>   *Look what I can do when pushed too far.*

People race
inland.
Our son walks
from the West Village
to the Upper East Side.
Families return to slabs
of concrete, their homes
somersaulting in the waves.
Neighborhoods smolder.

I Wear Our Love Like a Sweater

When I want to remember
where we came from,
I sink into its aged wool,
reach in the pocket
for a long-ago left
sketch on the back of a receipt—
a prolonged kiss in a Mazda RX-7
after a late Sunday-night movie,
a mad dash of snowflakes
erasing parking lot lines.

I Know This

Somewhere along Route 92
between steep slopes and raging waters,
wind carries apologies
for sins—past, present, future—up and over
helmet haunting deaf ears.

Exhale. Again.

CURVES AHEAD.

We swerve
around missed games, forgotten conversations
like the letting go of a childhood
blanket, high school trophies, a college sweatshirt.

See beyond culm banks
and a hollow earth to tree tops cradling sun,
a marriage built young,
now willing itself to survive.

CAUTION.

Slow speed to take next left deftly.
Exit Six and *The Sad Café* wait around the corner
from a home sweet and settling
where I shed my mother's mold
like layers of skin sloughing.

Speed is born on pavement.
Gears shift. The bridge connects two
lost in woods along the river.

Crying Summer

I cried you to sleep
every night
as we wove our bodies like a braid
on the tattered day bed.

An entire season sequestered
on the sleeping porch,
a treehouse nestled among evergreens
taller and fuller than that first July
you brought me to your family's lake house
when I slept on the porch
with your girl cousins,
and you slept in a tent
with the boys
two stories below.

We fished,
breathed in fire-pit smoke,
played volleyball,
and eavesdropped on cricket chatter.

Now, the porch screens are no longer taut,
floor planks are coated with pollen
and chipped paint.

It cradled our history
as conversations best-not-seen-in-daylight flowed
into the dark space between us.

Tears ran
until the moon and sun crossed,
kissing briefly in a metal sky.

It's been so many years,
I almost forgot
how the edge of memory dissolves.

Several decades
are the bridge to an aging house moored
between a homecoming and a goodbye.

Your father gone this year,
your inheritance,
the sleeping porch,
the safest place for confessing our sins.

Hard to Swallow

I used to have a steel-plated,
Teflon-coated stomach.

ER visits for flying leap off couch
chin landing on coffee table.
Razor scooter tripped by rock,
eye meets handle bar.
Breath stolen
by mid-air soccer collision.

I washed sheets of vomit by night-light glow,
counted minutes in clouds
of phlegm-filled midnights on winter's front porch,
wrapped in a cocoon of blankets.

I weathered moods
dark as a thunderstorm,
silent treatments protected by closed doors,
worried in the mountains of home
for sons finding their lives
in the shadows of skyscrapers.

Years chipped at the Teflon coating.
The steel rusted.
My stomach spasms,
esophagus clenches.
Messages from a dorm RA.
Date rape in south Wilkes-Barre.

Female genital mutilation in Africa.
A toddler gone missing on a European vacation.
Members of my cousin's unit killed in Afghanistan.

The acid rises higher.
It's hard to swallow.

I choke on water,
gag every morning
on the tiniest of vitamins.

Imaginary Numbers

My son tries again to explain discreet math,
the *I* of imaginary numbers and how when squared
they create a negative.

I get lost in the code of his foreign language
and answer in metaphor and allusion.

I sit on the soft leather sofa
where he's played video games for hours,
where we've spent years
watching movies and golf matches.

I picture him on his apartment's rooftop
leaning back in a lawn chair.
His feet clad in Samba soccer shoes
push against a brick ledge.

Spanish, Kru, Creole, and English,
car horns, and squeak of backyard gate
float upward. Above him,
the Bronx sky is a vast canvas.

Winter

You say I'm trying too hard,
tending the fire in the ancient fireplace.

With toe of your work boot, you tamp
embers jumping onto the carpet
to escape my control.

But where will we be
when the fire's light
turns dark, charred wood cools,
the house turns to ash?

Quilting

I stitched our story,
a kaleidoscope of curves
and corners; sunburst
and ocean waves.

A chance meeting at Costa Drugs. That spectacular fight.
The phone call from Venice. The beginnings of our sons.
Midnight words. Highways of silence.
My line breaks. Your flugelhorn.
The day I broke your heart. The night you shocked mine.

When my crying
wakes you
and the alarm is hours away,
I will teach you to read the quilt
like Braille, knowing the way back
is always by touch.

Mushroom Soup

I began cooking when it was just the two of us. Spicy chicken chili and hearty white-bean soup. I made Sundays-at-Grandma's meatloaf and mashed potatoes. Italian wedding soup minus the ingredients I dislike. Things I could drown our empty nest in. The Sunday before Thanksgiving after the August when the tree on the property line turned red, and my hair grey, I stood at the kitchen window and hand-pureed mushroom soup. Leaves wrestled in the yard and the sun wrapped itself in empty branches. Silence whirred like Santa Ana winds. I wanted the clamor again. Our youngest searing steak on the stove. Our oldest pacing the kitchen as he described the latest concert he attended. You, with hands on my hips, pushing my hair to the side to run your lips down my neck.

Just a Ride

Silvery metal
and polished chrome
radiate in the afternoon sun.

The engine warms
our cool bodies.

We ride along the river's edge
through evergreen mountains.

Leaning in,
we learn each other's curves.

Dizzy with speed
I hold tighter
and wonder why
I was ever afraid.

Make Time

Cool relief of cucumber
mask applied to her face.

Close eyes. Breathe in.

Salve calms skin,
seeps in like a slow
drink of water in July.

Saturday's play date,
the evening's dinner menu,
and her son's missed
homework assignments
electrify her thoughts.

Release.

Experienced hands begin their
work. Her shoulders let down,
neck sinks into softness. Stress leaks
from fingertips like dew drops
off an early April tulip.

Relax.

She forgot milk and flavored
coffee. She needs to call
the dentist and the painter

needs a color decision,
burnt umber or crimson sky,
by tomorrow.

Remember.

Hot stones find their place
along her spine,
and her mind empties
of commitments, problems with no
solutions, random thoughts. She
absorbs heat to cache away for
the long season ahead.

Abandon

He speaks of meanness,
a streak as wide and deep
as the nearby river,
its swift current pushing chunks of ice.

Bare trees stand straight
against charcoal sky
and wait for sun to cut across frozen,
flat land.

Wind lashes
without knowing the depths it reaches.

Words sting and open
the last light of a frigid night dawning.

She doesn't feel the blood
rising to the surface,
doesn't know
passion until the skin bruises blue,
and purple speckles pool along her neck.

How quickly it turns
from summer sweetness,
a rush of tides,
to wild winter wickedness.

Charcoal sky opens.
Snow flurries.

Winter stands still.

You Held My Hand,

anonymous and free
in a city not our own.
You took me to experience

it stark, stripped, bare.
Wool hats and fleece gloves—ashen,
charcoal like old New York snow.

No one knew us—just two strangers
trying to keep warm.
Snow fell in large wet balls

dancing with skeleton trees
before it settled
on pavement over the brown grass.

You held my hand
fleece against fleece,
the heat escaped. We talked

about redwood forests,
the distance to the center of the earth,
poetry and one-act plays.

When we stopped
to admire the gates,
a display of art and architecture,

whimsy and hype, you pulled me close.
Never before
a slow public kiss, never again,
you held my hand.

Second Chance

Late last winter when single-digit
temperatures overstayed their welcome
and thick frost clung to windows, the agile
snow swirled through a door opened
then closed. Wrapped in the luxury
of four insulated walls, words simmered
while second chances smoldered. Blindly
diving in, they sifted through the silt of their life
and salvaged discarded secrets,
the aromas of memory,
the hunger from a day spent apart.
Melting snow pushed away the past,
rekindled the barren hearth.

.

Fire Wood

He still prefers her voice,
a velvety alto, to the silence. When she says

There is always time, his mind goes to work,
a mental sketch. The rise and fall of his

arms splits wood so splinters
become embers. He contemplates

the image, pauses to sketch,
folds paper into pocket for later.

His breath heaves into fall air. In the evening,
he climbs plank stairs to the studio. His body

curls over work bench, the sketch tacked
to its surface. Intricate handiwork and metal.

One precious stone. Her voice,
It's never too late.
His back kept warm by an ancient stone

fireplace, its pops and hisses dwindle
as night turns to morning.

Flow

I run to the house on the hill,
white clapboard, slate shingles,
a yard speckled with spruce and pine.

I slip through the back
door, lock it behind me,
like it is my own.

Light from the basement
throws shadows across
beadboard and stainless

steel. I climb down the stairs,
duck under a bowed oak beam.
He works the wheel, spins clay,

muddy water runs to his elbows.
With a nod he motions to the small
stool next to him. I sit and words

flow as his hands pull up
the piece, shaping the walls.
He never takes his eyes from the wheel,

its speed smooth, no wobbles,
like a dreidel across glass. He leaves
streaks when he wipes his hand

on faded jeans, reaches to brush
my hair away from my eyes.

Stay as long as you like,
he says.
But take something when you go.

Sign Language

After H.L. Hix's "Reasons"
and Kim Addonizio's "First Poem for You"

When I sing *Please*,
you shiver.

After your fingertips map my palm,
my skin craves your electricity.

Since a double-dare overcame fear,
fear led to adventure.

Because a whispered want tickles,
I want to be remembered as bold.

Before rock trounces scissors,
some moments hatch memories.

Where you sketched nirvana,
the artist etched skin.

Once love excuses lust,
lust ignites love.

Sinew

If I knew you would sprint across the tracks,
jump the crumbling stone wall,
run through the Victorian's weed-punctuated yard,
climb the rusted fire escape,
push up my bedroom window,
its aging panes rattled by freight-train rumble,
just enough to slide in your runner's body,
and tuck me under you by light of the midnight moon,
then I wouldn't have had to cry
so many years over my fall from grace.

Parallel Text on an
Indian Summer Day

My students dissect Mark Antony's speech,
and a girl who never raises her hand
and never speaks above a whisper
explains his use of repetition, wonders
aloud why Brutus didn't stay to keep an eye on him.

A boy, who is counting the days to graduation,
likes Antony's sarcasm
and how he wept with emotional
appeal to sway the plebs.

These middle schoolers
whose voices span octaves in a single sentence,
whose moods shift quicker than a minute hand
take time to hear Shakespeare's voice,
to hunt parallel text for understanding.

They count each other's lines
from the previous day,
argue over which parts to read.

That evening,
the sun leaves the sky earlier than yesterday,
and a chill descends.

I once made a living writing persuasive copy,
but over dinner I forget Shakespeare's lessons.
Misplaced words and missing antecedents.
Pertinent facts omitted. No trace
of logical sequence in my story.

You look at me over the edge
of your reading glasses from across a table set for two
that now seems as long as a medieval banquet.

My diction is off, so I begin again chanting
I'm sorry, I'm sorry, but you only ask,
What do you want me to do about the past?

A Different Kind of Storm

Leaves covered their faces.
Branches bobbed and snapped
to the ground.

A night of sideways rain,
ponds pooled
in lowest part of garden.
Cucumbers and chipmunks
nearly drowned.

Lightning drew the sky
to an electric dance,
too beautiful to look away.

Thunder,
percussive energy against walls.
Window panes shuddered
and curtains quivered.

By morning, the storm evaporated.
Drenched lawns dried
and temperatures rose in the mid-day light.

A day of humid pauses
languished in the heat
of unexpected summer secrets
released into an uncharted forest.

Then, a different kind of storm steeping.

Circling Love

His hands
> explore
> shoulder, arm, small of back

> draw
> slow circles,
> a modern waltz.

She succumbs
> to pressure
> of electric fingers

> and questions. Her declarative yes
> dances
> into shared space.

It Began as a Summer Whim

You twirled a strand of my sun-bleached hair
and pulled me into sea-salted lips and tongue.
Sparkles of rain sizzled on our arms.

My voice was the trill of Sirens that loosened
our moorings.

We wrote the opening lines of our story on sand,
dove deeper into the channels of stormy waves,
didn't know, or care, how far from shore
we had drifted until the clouds separated
to wisps of cotton, the silvery light
of a waning gibbous moon.

Years of moon cycles later
you are still magnetic,
a water sign who never strayed far from salt,
but I'm a paper doll
land-locked in someone else's house.

Storytelling

1.

Erotic,
he whispers
and tucks a strand of hair
behind her ear.

She rolls with the word
the space   between
closes a final pause

spins and dives,
then rises like steam
from the surface
of a lake after a storm.
The space   between
evaporates.

2.

Love,
she begins,
tucking the phone
between ear and shoulder.

Are you alone?

The trees here are encased in ice,
their limbs bend to touch
the frozen lake. Fishermen
are building an igloo.

Inside, the cat
kneads the empty bed,
mews for a return, a plea
for the missing.

3.

Stop,
he says.

Instead, she flows like notes
from the bell of a horn
a stream of melody,
ethnic harmony, old
bow crosses strings.
A co-mingling blossoms.

4.

Enough,
she pleads.

A half moon shivers
behind harmonious clouds.

Meant to say enough,
a held gaze folds yes
into a crimson envelope.

5.

Cross.
He suggests
the line again.

She unravels a reckoning,
which she doesn't want.

She doesn't want
to see crimson drops
from a thumb prick
he presses to his lips,
eyes unmoving, his tongue warm.

Water Dream

I dreamt of you
in blue-green waters
swimming electricity
in the air. Hazy questions hover
afraid to touch

your lips. Buoyed by weight
of emotions you push
a foaming crest toward me.

White waves turn over
thoughts like driftwood.
The waters plead.

Stay longer.

Pictures

1.

She handles my breasts
like a newborn baby.

I'm sorry the plastic is cold.
This will be uncomfortable.
He wants more pictures.

I stare at the wall,
blank as a field
cloaked in snow.

Click. Click. Click.

2.

His words are the sharp point
of an icicle pricking my skin
as he taps the image with tip of his pen.

A puzzle . . . looks benign
but acts
differently.

The pictures light up
mysterious snowflakes
dancing in an onyx sky.

Two years ago, scattered flurries,
now a silent squall
with a two percent chance of a blinding blizzard.

3.

The needle punctures my skin,
bears through tissue
and pictures that guide
the surgeon's hand
to swirling snowflakes.

I imagine the geometry of their shapes
coalescing into a snowball
and I slide out of control
off the slippery slope
into a forest of ice-encrusted pines.

Diamond dust shimmers
in the thinnest of air.

Winter Conversation

Under a full moon, dim stars blur
as if brushed-stroked across the black
sky. She idles in a dark car. Shivering
from winter's edge, she rests her head
against the frosted window, watches new
snow skittering across icy drifts. Phone
cradled on her shoulder she closes her eyes
to listen, spring just far enough away to want.

Current

Months after the flood
we drive along Wyoming Avenue.
Winter clouds clothe then unclothe a half moon.
The wind nudges the car, its chill
bites for the first time
in this unseasonable season.

Mounds of debris still line the curb
block after block. Where were the walls
of dirt, grass, and rock
when this town needed them?
When the heat of summer still clung
to September and the river left its banks?

I know families who watched venomous water
barge in, an intruder
who upended daily life, stole heirlooms,
clogged furnaces, left behind swollen walls,
and a carpet of mud.

They trudged through sludge to search
for remnants of their lives
now divided into before and after:
a grandmother's sodden fur coat,
children's muck-smeared artwork,
kitchen chairs, their legs bruised.

At each red light, I stare at the mounds:
an antique dining table, mildewed
and warped, bikes with rusted
tire spokes, a swing set reduced
to Tinker Toys that mourn the past.

I imagine the water's path, its brown
rage carrying trees and buildings
downsized to firewood as they hit
the bellies of bridges.

One house's porch shimmers
with white lights while its neighbor
is a ghost, its insides hollow and drying out.

Imprint

Smooth curve of hip
is the artist's canvas.

From expert hands flow
perfect eye for color
and fill in between
lines of life's imperfections.

Blank stretch
no longer lonely,
but tiny star bursts
orbiting a slender
crescent moon.

Surface of skin
vibrates. The needle
hurts. Don't let them
tell you otherwise.

The Scholar

His hair, graying just above
the ears, wraps likes parentheses
around his eyes. His glasses,
black, rectangular plastic
fit his strong face.

He wears a blue blazer, steamed
tailored white shirt, and khaki
pants, creased down to his penny
loafers. He knew
what he was talking about.

As he speaks,
he spins his wedding ring,
a simple gold band,
around his finger.

He is the kind of guy
I would've dated in college.
Leaning against a banister,
he would peel the label from a bottle of Heineken
as he quoted Dylan Thomas
and couples squeezed by us on their way upstairs.
I would have fallen right there.

Today, he talks marketing and education,
about home, his faith, and his young girls.
Outside the conference room window,
spring arrives in a bouquet of greens,
pink and purple punctuated dots. For a brief minute

I wish I met him twenty years ago
at a frat party
talking about poetry
while couples passed us,
their fingers entwined
in each other's belt loops.

Kith

The party always began in the back yard—
        coolers filled with ice, beer and soda,
        burgers spitting into lighter fluid and charcoal.

A circle of lawn chairs with frayed webbing
        held aunts in bell bottoms and halter tops,
        their gossip only interrupted to yell at children

running with sparklers in hand. Inside the Victorian,
        grandfather sat for hours at an old upright
        against the back wall of dining room, a line

of Budweiser cans sweat circles into the wood's grain.
        Playing by ear, he ran through his song list
        always ending with "Danny Boy" or "When Irish

Eyes are Smiling" just as the marathon game of Jeopardy
        fired up around the mahogny table, siblings
        and spouses divided into teams with colored

clickers in one hand, Coors Light and Camels in the other.
        As the game entered its third hour, arguments rose
        over Potent Potables and who forgot to shout

answers as questions. The kids a patchwork den carpet
        using each other as pillows, the youngest in charge
        of cranking the volume on the console to make

Gilda Radner's laugh win over dining-room noise.
        Cigarette smoke coiled, hung above the kids
        before escaping through open windows

dissolving into the dark backyard while mosquitoes
        skittered against dusty screens, always
        a frenetic dance toward unreachable light.

Family

She is late, but there's something
about the frenetic swirls, the brown
haze filling the air that makes
her slow down and park to watch.

The winds blow
dust, litter, remnants of winter
in the streets, a rainless spring storm
kick up a fight in the afternoon heat.

New-born blossoms torn from fragile limbs
spin, a restless rustle of something
not quite right, haunts in the near dusk.

She realizes her uncle will
not be here when the leaves change
their colors come fall, a late diagnosis offers
no hope. The year she was seven

he navigated his Seventies van, dark blue, late at night
through an ice storm, wheels spinning the hill,
she and her sister stretched out
in the carpeted back,

their mother turned to hush their chatter.
He was wild and angry,
a hard-drinking world traveler who then said
It's never too late to change. Twenty-five

years later he settled in a quiet life of giving,
tending the garden with care, the turning
of soil and the new leaves each season.

She lets the car idle, doesn't care if she's late
for an event she doesn't want to attend,
watches the trees bend to the winds
blow a chant for the dying.

Roots

I'm not made of mountains or valleys.
There's no stench of river mud in my hair
or coal dusting my family albums.
My grandfather played stickball on the streets
of Jersey City, sang an Irish Lullaby to court
my grandmother at St. Patrick's in Elizabeth.
He went to work the brewery line, dormant
hops and barley sprouted in his blood, flowed
freely into our clan. Some turned their backs
on its bitter taste and yeasty smell, in others
it brewed and boiled staining our house
for generations. But, my parents escaped,
flew us far from those shadows. Yes, I
was transplanted several times over on plains
and in a city below sea level before landing
in these mountains. I grew roots here, married
local, cultivated lives, began to call it home
for better or worse.

Hibernia

A cold downpour in early autumn
stills the evening commute. Rows of brake

lights four wide blur in the drenched
dusk. It's a homecoming

of sorts, this detour to Hibernia. Diners
run deep in us Jersey girls, no matter

how long the separation. Toddlers
in tow, we sink into a weathered booth,

its tabletop worn. Steam rises from matzo
ball soup. Fresh romaine, tomatoes, feta,

cucumbers, and olives. Thick chocolate shakes.
A matriarch never forgets to tether family ties

to comfort food and childhood memory.
But now, tonight, with a blocked interstate

outside a foggy window, after a journey to respect
a dying generation, new lines are tied

in the old Hibernia diner. A return home,
yes. Diners run deep in Jersey girls.

Heat Lightning

Two Irish sisters sit in white wicker
and watch the evening sky shimmer and glow.

A half century ago,
they were teenage girls
with flipped hair and skirts
inching above the knee.

Decades ago, they protected children
from backyard alligators and Palmetto
bug shadows, cracked coconuts, and saved
marriages on sizzling Florida concrete.

Now, they are grandmothers prone
to weeping and hour-long goodbyes,
and they laugh the same way
at the same unfunny things.

As lightning flirts with the darkening sky,
stories come fast, spilling
a basket of family lore. An aunt and a mom
feeding us our history, spoonfuls
of melodic syllables compose our family's Celtic song.

Seaside Heights, 2011

After prayer and incense at Mass,
a police-escorted procession,
and an Irish family goodbye,
the Atlantic pulls you East.

You walk the weathered boards of your childhood
passed Lucky Leo's, thud of Skeeball and jangle
of arcade music, a portal to Saturdays
counting tickets and picking prizes.
The air is alive with Italian sausage sizzle,
pizza grease, and the tang of vinegar fries.

In the Berkeley Sweet Shop,
you escape the November wind
to warm your nose and fingers,
buy creamy chocolate fudge
that will be gone by the time
you cross the Pennsylvania border.

The late afternoon draws geometric shadows
on the wide swath of beach,
polka-dotted with people.

You meet your cousin at the tip of a triangle,
walk dry sand to wet,
and your words tangle with the wind,
then dissolve in the spray.

That day, your grandmother
is the Atlantic,
a blue horizon, an infinite wake,
white-capped water that spirals
and folds and ebbs.
A circular tide
carrying all memory of the past,
all the secrets of your future.

Under the Stairs

Cousins sit cross-legged, knees
touching in a closet,
playing Life.

A single light bulb casts shadows
on career choices as we race

around the board. We plan
future weddings, share secrets

of a ceremony on a grassy knoll,
honeymooning in a rain forest

tree house, wearing a champagne-
colored dress. We promise, sealed

by a pinky swear, to be bridesmaids
for each other. In the kitchen

our parents talk about road trips,
Bourbon Street, job promotions.

We whisper in pig Latin about Shaun
Cassidy, Catholic school uniforms,

living far from home
until they call us for dinner.

Warinanco Park

Ducks preen feather
with flat beaks and turn
slow circles, orange webs
churn the water.

In matching blue Keds
we skid to a stop
at the pond's muddy edge.
The bread,
rough as sandpaper,
in our hands, hits

the surface. Some bob
for food, others waddle
ashore to pluck
from finger tips.
Empty-handed,
we race to the bench

where Grandmother
waits, legs crossed,
cigarette poised
between index
and middle fingers.
Watching
behind green-tinted
sunglasses, she blows

smoke rings above our
heads. We beg for more.

NorthSouth

In backyard gardens
we hide and seek . . .

blue wisteria,
full-bloom magnolia.

I climb the fence.

Ready or not
                    I jump,

                    picket catches
                    my shoelace
                    and I'm falling.

Lucille finds me hanging
upside down,

hair skimming ferns
            below. She tugs
at my shoelace, and

I somersault into the ferns,

            cool, damp.

                    Lucille lands
                    behind me

and the chase
begins again

around the weeping
willow, through honeysuckle.

We weave in and out of her mom's
        bamboo garden,
            collapse on her porch swing.

                    Faces streaked
                    with dirt, we gulp
                    lemonade, wipe
                    our mouths on t-shirts.
Swinging slowly, our tennis shoes
glide over common ground.

Evening Prayer

Morning.

She tends the seeds with a light
step humming, a smile turns
up at dirt staining hands,
sweat trickling down small of back.

The rain comes, quick and cool,
she turns her face to the sky
eyes closed, feet planted.

Early afternoon.

Sky wide open,
an ocean so deep
she could dive in and never surface.

Humid air heavy with waiting.
The weight of harvest never far
from her thoughts, her long
days push against the heat
rising from the field.

Late afternoon.

She ploughs the field,
a crisp wind at her back.
She scrubs the last of summer's
earth from hands, black water circling

the drain. Later, meandering
a wooden path, she cries alone,
the scent of fall around every bend.

Evening.

In the dark, cold seeps. Every crevice,
a draft. She goes to bed with a dreamless
sleep. This season of mourning does not
forgive what might be on the other side.

Outstretched arms, she asks
for a prayer, the strength of moonlight,
a shower of stars cascading.

White Noise

Kitchen faucet drips
to rhythm of the gurgling fridge.
Water climbs aging veins of house.
Furnace jump-starts.
Dishwasher whooshes through cycle.

Cat purrs while curled under window.
Trumpet music streams.
Son's muffled voice behind
bedroom door as he talks
to his girlfriend two thousand miles away.

Outside, a crunchy layer of snow
on dead grass. Thick ice coats
windshields of Passats and Jettas
in driveway.

With the thaw so far away,
I forget what daffodils smell like.

6:45 Train

She drinks the bright warmth
and waits, always waits,
for tomorrow
and the late-train whistle
signaling his arrival.

(An idea catches her attention
and draws her closer to movement.)

He transforms with each mile
while replaying
their early morning goodbye.

As he steps onto the solid wood platform,
it never occurs to him
she's done waiting.

Acknowledgements

The author wishes to acknowledge the editors of the following magazines, anthologies, and journals where these poems originally appeared, sometimes in different versions:

Connecticut River Review: "Bonfire"
San Pedro River Review: "Empty Cars" and "Seaside Heights 2011"
Potluck: "Abandon" and "Parallel Text"
Willows Wept Review: "NorthSouth"
Word Fountain: "Current" and "Winter Conversation"
Cohort Review: "Flow"
East Meets West, American Writers Review: "Simmer," "Storytelling," and "Vacation"
Everyday Escape Poems anthology (SwanDive Publishing): "Heat Lightning," "Hibernia," and "Roots"
Clear Poetry: "Sinew"
Poetry in Transit: "Explorer" and "Water Dream"
River of Earth and Sky: Poems for the 21st Century (Blue Light Press): "Pictures"
Home anthology (Mainstreet Rag, spring 2015): "Carpet Cleaning"

I offer my heartfelt thanks, gratitude, and appreciation to the following:

Jessica Kristie for welcoming me into the Winter Goose gaggle and for your expert guidance throughout the process. James Koukis for your editing skills, support, and copyediting collaboration. Loren Kleinman for your editing eye and for guiding me toward Winter Goose Publishing. Mischelle Anthony and Bill Black. Our hours spent huddled over stories and poems in Zummo's, Le Manhattan Bistro, and Tomato Bar & Bistro have meant the world to me and helped move many of these poems down the right path. Diane Frank for your thoughtful comments and guidance sent across the country via cyberspace. Christine Gelineau, Tony Morris, and Neil Shepard for years of mentorship and friendship. Mike Lennon for encouraging me to apply for a Norman Mailer Center Workshop in Brooklyn, and Quincy Troupe for his expert insight and editing suggestions during that one-week workshop. Bonnie Culver, Bill Schneider, Joyce Anzalone, my cohort, and the entire Wilkes University MA/MFA Creative Writing community for being my second family. Rashidah Ismaili for your encouragement that I forge ahead on my writing path and your firm insistence that I apply to the Wilkes program. Barb Taylor, Ronda Bogart, Nancy McKinley, Taylor Polites, Laurie Loewenstein, Jackie Fowler, Vicki Mayk, Lori A. May, and Brian Fanelli for true friendship and enthusiastic cheerleading. My parents, twin sister, brother-in-law, niece and nephew for your unconditional support and love. My aunts, uncles, and countless cousins for attending readings and showing interest in my writing journey.

Lastly, but most importantly, a million thanks and endless love to Jeff, Ryan, and Evan. This book wouldn't exist without you.

About the Author

Photo by Nathan Summerlin

Dawn Leas is a Pushcart Prize nominated poet. Her work can be found in numerous publications, including *Literary Mama and Southern Women's Review*, and her chapbook, *I Know When to Keep Quiet*, was released in 2010 by Finishing Line Press. Dawn holds an MFA in Creative Writing from Wilkes University, where she is currently assistant to the president, and is a contributing editor at *Poets' Quarterly and The ThePoetry*.

Notes

Crying Summer: Sleeping porches are screened-in, secluded rooms, often on the second floor of a home (not a front entranceway to a house). They gained popularity in the early 20th century before air-conditioning as an escape from stuffy, hot indoor rooms, which still offered protection from pesky bugs.

I Know This: "The Sad Café" is the title of an Eagles song on *The Long Run* album.

Slipstream: This poem was written in response to "*Zooropa* Turns 20" by Ryan Leas for www.sterogum.com. It borrows "slipstream," "dream out loud," "fly," "map," "uncertainty," and "what do you want" from the song's lyrics.

Sign Language: This poem began as a graduate-school writing exercise that melded the forms, structures, content, and themes of two poems for which I chose H.L. Hix's "Reasons" and Kim Addonizio's "First Poem for You."

CPSIA information can be obtained at www.ICGtesting.com
Printed in the USA
BVOW08s0830120416

443911BV00002B/8/P